Diary of a Somebody

John Lahr's successful dramatization of *The Orton Diaries*
chronicles the last eight months of Joe Orton's life, his growing
theatrical celebrity and the corresponding punishing effect it had
on his relationship with his friend and mentor Kenneth H~~a~~
who murdered him on August 9, 1967

'Orton's diaries put us on the r
boisterous talent at its zenith. F
man acutely observant of the hi
strangely oblivious to the hyster
Halliwell'.

Edmund White, *The Sunday Times*

'The world owes John Lahr a great deal for the work he has done
on behalf of Orton. The diaries are really quite extraordinary . . .
a pleasure to read something in which one can hear such a
distinctive, intelligent voice . . . such assured literary judgments
uncluttered by the conventional standards of the literary
establishment'.

Jonathan Miller

JOHN LAHR was born in Los Angeles in 1941. He is the author
of the biographies of Joe Orton, *Prick Up Your Ears*, and of his
father, the comedian Bert Lahr, *Notes on a Cowardly Lion*, as well
as a full-length critical study of the plays of Noel Coward. He has
published three collections of essays on theatre: *Acting Out
America*, *Astonish Me* and *Automatic Vaudeville* for which the
London Review of Books called him the 'F.R. Leavis of the
performing arts'. He has also edited *The Orton Diaries* and written
two novels: *The Autograph Hound* and *Hot to Trot*. He is at work
on his third novel and writes a monthly theatre column for *Vogue*.

The front cover illustration is by Paul Davies.

JOHN LAHR

Diary of a Somebody

Based on
The Orton Diaries

METHUEN DRAMA

A METHUEN MODERN PLAY

First published in Great Britain as a Methuen paperback original
in 1989 by Methuen Drama, Michelin House, 81 Fulham Road,
London SW3 6RB

Diary of a Somebody © 1989 John Lahr and The Estate of Joe
Orton

Printed and bound in Great Britain by Cox and Wyman, Reading.

British Library Cataloguing in Publication Data
Lahr, John, *1941–*
    Diary of a somebody
    I. Title
    812′.54

    ISBN 0-413-61180-9

CAUTION
This play is fully protected by copyright. All rights whatsoever in
this play are strictly reserved and application for performance etc.
should be made before rehearsal to Margaret Ramsay Limited of
14a Goodwin's Court, St. Martin's Lane, London WC2N 4LL.
No performance may be given unless a licence has been obtained.

In Memory of

JAMES AND NICHOLAS LAHR

God bless them

Foreword

This play was written in happy collaboration with its fine director, Jonathan Myerson. He has mounted the show in its various versions at the National Theatre, The King's Head, the West End, and on national tour. I salute him at the end of our exciting, sometimes rollicking, adventure.

Orton's Diary, which he entitled DIARY OF A SOMEBODY, was written in the last eight months of his life and chronicles his first real taste of literary success. Orton's agent, Peggy Ramsay, had first suggested a diary in 1965. But then, with Orton's first full-length play, *Entertaining Mr. Sloane* (1964), having recently closed on Broadway after thirteen performances and with his second play, *Loot*, (1965), a notorious flop in its original production, Orton had no faith in his own future. The success of *Loot*'s revival in 1966 emboldened Orton. Just four months before, he had been threatening to quit the theatre: 'I'm really quite capable of carrying this out,' he wrote to Peggy Ramsay, 'I've always admired Congreve who, after the absolute failure of *The Way of the World*, just stopped writing.'

Before *Loot*'s success, Orton was promising: now he was suddenly major. His literary style and his life acquired a new amperage. In the short period in which he was writing the diary, Orton also wrote *Funeral Games*, a ghoulish capriccio about faith and justice; rewrote his first play, *The Ruffian on the Stair* (1963) and *The Erpingham Camp* (1965) for the Royal Court double-bill, *Crimes of Passion*; completed the screenplay *Up Against It* for the Beatles; and wrote his farce masterpiece *What the Butler Saw*.

When Orton's luck changed, so did his relationship with Kenneth Halliwell, whom he had met and moved in with during his first term at RADA in 1951. To Orton, a callow lad from Leicester, Halliwell was promise incarnate. He had everything Orton lacked: a car, a library, an education. He also had a good line in literary chat. Halliwell took control of Orton, educating him and filling him with dreams of glory. After a decade of literary failure and a six month prison sentence in 1962 for (comically) defacing library books, Orton broke through. He'd found his voice. Halliwell never did.

Diary of a Somebody picks up the story when the power in the two men's relationship had shifted irrevocably in Orton's favour. Orton had the big bank balance, the big name, and the big future. Halliwell was, as he wrote, 'Secretary to Joe Orton'.

The Diary was provocative to Halliwell not just because it recorded Orton's promiscuity, but because it failed to recount his own legitimate demands in his quarrels with Orton. This dramatization incorporates letters, taped material from sources from my biography of Orton, *Prick Up Your Ears*, literary fragments and psychiatric reports.

Many people have played an important part in helping to bring Orton's life and Diary to the public. I thank them warmly again at the conclusion of this seventeen year project – the Orton Estate, Peggy Ramsay, Nick Hern, Paul Sidey, the late Kenneth Williams, and most especially Anthea Lahr, for her insights into Halliwell's predicament, for her brutal blue pencil and for her friendship these many years.

John Lahr
23 November 1988

Diary of a Somebody was first performed in a one-act version at the Cottesloe Theatre, the National Theatre on December 1st, 1986 with the following cast:

JOE ORTON	John Sessions
KENNETH HALLIWELL	Bruce Alexander
OSCAR LEWENSTEIN, HUSBAND ON BUS, GEORGE, UNDERTAKER, KENNETH CRANHAM, FREDDIE, MR. CORDEN, WALTER SHENSON, MIDDLE-AGED MAN, BUTLER, PAUL McCARTNEY, RAILWAY OFFICIAL ON BUS, FIRST LIBYAN, LIBYAN CLERK, LIBYAN MANAGER, PETER WILLES, KENNETH WILLIAMS, NIGEL, MOHAMMED LARBI, CYPRIOT, and CLERKISH MAN	Richard Denning
WIFE ON BUS, NICHOLA WEBB, MRS. CORDEN, E. WELTHORPE (MRS.), and MRS. LEWENSTEIN	Lynn Farleigh
BUS CONDUCTRESS, LEONIE ORTON, MISS BOYNES, WOMAN ON BUS, J.P.H. JOY and SHEILA BALLANTINE	Caroline Webster

Directed by Jonathan Myerson
Designed by Gillian Daniell

The play was subsequently produced in this full-length version on 7th April, 1987, at the King's Head Theatre Club. The cast was as follows:

JOE ORTON	Oliver Parker
KENNETH HALLIWELL	Ian Bartholemew
OSCAR LEWENSTEIN, HUSBAND ON BUS, GEORGE, UNDERTAKER, MR. ORTON, PETER WILLES, KENNETH CRANHAM, FREDDIE, MR. CORDEN, WALTER SHENSON, MIDDLE-AGED MAN, BUTLER, PAUL McCARTNEY, PETER BROWN, BRIAN	

EPSTEIN, RAILWAY OFFICIAL ON
BUS, AIRPORT LIBYAN, LIBYAN
CLERK, LIBYAN MANAGER,
KENNETH WILLIAMS, NIGEL, BOY,
GEORGE GREEVES, MOHAMMED
COPPERTONE, LARBI, STREET
VENDOR, CYPRIOT, DOCTOR, and
CLERKISH MAN FROM HOVE   Philip Lowrie
NICHOLA WEBB, MRS. CORDEN, WIFE
ON THE BUS, AUNT LUCY,
E. WELTHORPE (MRS.), FATIMA,
MAY HALLET and
MRS. LEWENSTEIN   Charlotte West-Oram
MISS BOYNES, BUS PASSENGER,
LEONIE ORTON, SHEILA
BALLANTINE, J.P.H. JOY, WOMAN
ON BUS, VIPSIL, AND EDITH   Caroline Webster

Directed by Jonathan Myerson
Designed by Gillian Daniell
Lighting by Dan Crawford

ACT ONE

As the audience enter, songs from 'Sgt. Pepper's Lonely Hearts Club Band' play.

The set comprises the ORTON-HALLIWELL *bedsitter: a single, claustrophobic room, the walls of which are covered in small reproductions of oil paintings cut from books and posters. It is a gigantic collage covering every available inch of wall space. Occasionally, the silhouette of a muscular man has been pasted over one great masterpiece or another. There is a single bed (two, if there is room – but in separate corners); a desk with a typewriter, papers and a telephone; a chair; a new television set in the corner; a radio; and little else. Basically, the set should be their Noel Road bedsitter as it was: ascetic – but for the wall coverings. If possible, it is useful to have a small corner or side-area, which is not collaged, but rather whitewashed, to represent other locales, most especially Tangiers. This area should also have a 'phone.*

Throughout the piece, the cast should remain on stage, sitting or standing at suitable places in the room, watching (though not obviously doing so) the action. They voice the dates.

The music and lights begin to fade, and, as they do so, all apart from HALLIWELL *enter. With the others voicing the dates,* JOE *addresses the audience. He is eighteen, has a slight Leicester accent, and is full of boyish naïveté.*

'Che Sera Sera' now plays.

VOICE A. May 15th, 1951.

JOE. Started at RADA. O bliss! An actor's life for me.

VOICE B. May 18th.

JOE. Digs in Gower Street. Such fun.

VOICE C. May 19th.

JOE. Oh the larks. Memo: Someone in the other class keeps looking at me.

VOICE A. May 21st.

JOE: Mr. Constable's special movement. Was eyed.

VOICE C. May 22nd.

JOE. Lawrence ate all the biscuits.

VOICE B. May 25th.

JOE: Met Ken and John at Charing Cross Road. Memo: I don't quite understand Ken.

VOICE A. May 27th.

JOE. Did nothing.

VOICE C. May 29th.

JOE. Lorrie ate all the nuts.

VOICE B. May 30th.

JOE. Lorrie ate all the bacon.

VOICE A. June 1st.

JOE. Met Ken and John again. This time with Rex Butler.

VOICE B. June 2nd.

JOE. Lorrie rang Ken. Memo: Am beginning to understand Ken.

VOICE C. June 4th.

JOE. Mr. Constable's movement. Well!

VOICE A. June 5th.

JOE. Lorrie ate all the cheese.

VOICE B. June 6th.

JOE. Lorrie ate all the cake.

VOICE A. June 7th.

JOE. Fuck Lorrie.

VOICE C. June 8th.

JOE. Met Ken. He invites us to live with him.

VOICE. June 9th.

JOE. Went to the pictures. Memo: I am puzzled.

VOICE C. June 10th.

JOE. Did nothing.

VOICE B. June 11th.

JOE. Must leave our digs.

VOICE A. June 12th.

JOE. Ken offers to share flat again.

VOICE C. June 13th.

JOE. I say No.

VOICE A. June 14th.

JOE. Ken offers again.

VOICE B. June 15th.

JOE. We accept because we must.

VOICE C. June 16th.

JOE. Move into Ken's flat.

VOICE B. June 17th.

JOE. Well!

VOICE. June 18th.

JOE. Well!!

VOICE C. June 19th.

JOE. Well!!!

VOICE B. June 20th, 1951.

JOE. The rest is silence.

The lights dim to spotlights on JOE *and* HALLIWELL. *They look at each other.* HALLIWELL *comes over and together they look through a script.* NICHOLA *helps* JOE *on with his fur coat.* HALLIWELL *gives* JOE *his denim cap. As the others withdraw and* OSCAR LEWENSTEIN *comes forward, the lights come up to full.*

JOE *is now thirty-three and wearing an imitation fur coat. 'Doo Wah Diddy Diddy' is playing on the radio.*

November 20th, 1966

LEWENSTEIN. You look very pretty in that.

JOE. Nichola said she'd buy me a coat – anything I wanted. Bought this for 13 pounds nineteen.

LEWENSTEIN. Very cheap.

JOE. She was appalled. But I've decided I look better in cheap clothes.

LEWENSTEIN. I wonder what the significance of that is?

JOE. I'm from the gutter. And don't you forget it, because I won't. (*To audience.*) The sound and the fury is over. *Loot* is a great success. After a decade of literary failure, living off National Assistance, my horizons no wider than our room – which is 16' by 12' – Joe Orton is the toast of the West End. I feel exhausted. Eighteen months of struggling to vindicate the honour of my play (my own is beyond vindication) has left me weak at the knees. We've scooped the pool with reviews –

HALLIWELL (*entering and turning off the radio*). Must we have this on?

JOE. Except for Mr Hobson of *The Times*. If one wants to be charitable, one could blame it on the sub-editors. Of course I'm not charitable.

HALLIWELL (*handing him the paper*). *The Mail's* sniffy.

JOE. Who cares? They don't sell one seat.

HALLIWELL. Letter from your publisher.

JOE. Give it.

HALLIWELL. For me.

JOE (*as HALLIWELL opens it*). Well?

HALLIWELL *reads but* NICHOLA *dictates it to her secretary.*

NICHOLA. Nothing is truer than to say that an editor is only good for certain authors, not all authors. I seem to be quite helpless where you are concerned. I haven't really got through your adaptation. I had to struggle to continue which I did with a kind of abstract anguish. Yours, et cetera . . .

HALLIWELL. 'And so the Gods distinction drew:
Good luck to Art,
A sod to you.'

JOE. I'm going down the shops . . . D'you want to – ?

HALLIWELL. I've just been down the shops. (*He starts to absorb himself in a collage.*) I've got things to do.

On his way out, JOE *passes the neighbours, after they have exchanged 'Good mornings' he introduces us to them.*

JOE (*to audience*). Miss Boynes from the floor below, and Mrs. Corden from the basement flat.

JOE *discreetly watches and listens to them.*

BOYNES. There's a lot of blue about lately.

Pause.

CORDEN. Yes. And there's a lot of green about too.

Pause.

BOYNES. And there's a lot of red. Have you noticed?

November 23rd

JOE (*to audience*). Got my hair cut at a new place in Knightsbridge. Cost a guinea for a style. It appears quite natural whilst in actual fact being incredibly artificial. A philosophy I approve of. Met my editor for lunch.

NICHOLA (*handing him the book*). The German edition.

JOE (*reading out the title (in German)*). *Amusieren Herr Sloane.* It'll pay for our holiday, I suppose. We're thinking about Libya this time.

NICHOLA. Tangiers has lost its charms, has it?

JOE. No, plenty of unspoilt bum still in Tangiers, but we're saving that for the Summer.

NICHOLA. You're lucky boys.

JOE. Did I tell you I'd been invited to the Lord Mayor's banquet?

NICHOLA. One of you should start a journal – au Gide.

JOE. A la Gide, surely?

NICHOLA. I'm sure I could talk the Board into publishing it.

JOE. Perhaps I am going to have an interesting life after all.

NICHOLA. Seriously. Talk this over with Ken. He's got writing talent but finds plots so difficult, and a diary would provide him with –

JOE. He's gone back to doing his collages. Says he's given up writing.

NICHOLA. Was it my letter?

JOE. Maybe it's better. He enjoys it, staying at home, piecing things together.

NICHOLA. Story of my life, darling. Piecing Enid Bagnold together at the moment.

JOE. *National Velvet.*

NICHOLA. The same. She's writing her autobiography. And she's really been fucked by some fascinating people. H.G. Wells, Frank Harris – she's living in Kipling's house.

JOE. Did Kipling – ?

NICHOLA. Almost certainly. But all these dead people are so boring. And Enid won't tell the truth about them.

JOE. As people grow older and have less to lose by telling the truth, they grow more discreet, not less. It's extraordinary.

NICHOLA. If only she'd tell us that old H.G. couldn't get it in. Or wore women's knickers. Or little Rudyard had a morbid fear of pubic hair. That would add to our knowledge of the man, wouldn't it?

JOE. Considerably.

NICHOLA. As it is, she'll just dither round the subject.

JOE. A lot of verbal asterisks.

NICHOLA. Exactly.

JOE (*to audience*). I didn't want to tell her I'd already started a diary. And mine will have no fucking asterisks. . . .

December 22nd

(*To audience*). The streets thronged with gay, fat women spending money like water. Just on the bus I counted five with bunches of plastic holly.

PASSENGER (*on the bus*). It's taken forty minutes to get from Vic to here.

WOMAN (*to her husband who is sitting next to her*). It's taken her forty minutes to get from Vic to here.

PASSENGER. I'm working Christmas Day.

WOMAN. She's working Christmas Day. Isn't it a shame?

PASSENGER. Oh, I don't mind.

WOMAN. She doesn't mind though. That's nice for her, isn't it?

Boxing Day

JOE (*to audience*). I began writing the second half of *What the Butler Saw*. Largely unmapped territory, successful at the moment. Likely to raise eyebrows in the Lord Chamberlain's office. I've had an excellent idea for continuing: Nick impersonates a policeman and arrests himself.

HALLIWELL (*handing back Orton's manuscript*). The first half is only thirty-two pages.

JOE. Single spaced.

HALLIWELL. It's not long enough. You need a slower build-up for the mayhem in the second act.

JOE. That's a depressing thought. I hope I can keep up sufficient frenzy until the end.

Pause.

We'll get there, won't we?

HALLIWELL *smiles, relaxed, nods yes.*

HALLIWELL (*referring to a line in the script*). This is wrong. 'Every sacred cow –'

JOE. '– pastures in England'? That's funny.

HALLIWELL. Too much. (*Pause.*) Too much.

JOE. . . . Yes.

He takes the pencil and crosses it out.

HALLIWELL. Madness is suddenly very fashionable. I see the film of *Marat-Sade*'s opening next week.

JOE. Actors recreating madness for paying customers. Let's look at mad people. Let's look at queer people. They have only to look in their mirrors.

HALLIWELL. You're writing about madness here.

JOE. There isn't a lunatic in sight. Just doctors and nurses being extravagantly melodramatic.

HALLIWELL. Lunatics are melodramatic.

JOE laughs.

JOE. That's a thought.

Phone rings. HALLIWELL answers it while Orton writes the line down.

HALLIWELL. Mr. Orton's secretary.

GEORGE. Hello, could I speak to John, please? (*He gives* JOE *the phone.*) Hello, John, it's George.

JOE. Hullo, George, how are you? How's Leicester?

GEORGE. Leonie asked me to ring to tell you your Mum died this morning. It was very quick. She had a heart attack.

JOE. He didn't say anything else. Father's just come out of hospital – he was run over by a car, but that won't make any difference to his brain – and is staying with my sister Leonie. (*To* HALLIWELL.) I'll go up to Leicester on Thursday. The funeral is Friday. (HALLIWELL *gives him the morning's mail,* JOE *opens it and tells* HALLIWELL.) From the editor of the Evening Standard . . . *Loot* has been voted Best Play of 1966. We've done it, Ken! (*They embrace.*) And I'm invited to the lunch at Quaglino's. It says 'and guest'?

HALLIWELL. Nothing on earth would get me to such a macabre affair. Why don't you ask Sheila. She's the best one in the cast, after all.

JOE (*to audience*). Then Leonie rang.

The 'phone rings.

LEONIE (*on 'phone*). Dad's gone back home. Sleeps in mum's bed with the corpse. After his accident, he can't piss straight and floods the lav with it. And I'm shocked by our Marilyn.

JOE (*on 'phone*). Why? What's she done?

LEONIE. Oh, you know, she behaves very ignorantly all around. When I told her Mum was dead, she said 'I'm not surprised'. Well, you know, what kind of remark is that? And Dougie's so upset.

JOE (*masking 'phone*). Remarkable how those without hearts when young suddenly develop them in later life. (*To* LEONIE.) I'll come tomorrow. Goodbye.

LEONIE 'Bye, then. (*She puts down the 'phone.*)

JOE (*to audience*). The coffin is downstairs now in the main living room, so it means watching television with death at one's elbow. A little too near the Freudian bone for comfort. And surprisingly reminiscent of *Loot*.

December 29th

Arrived in Leicester at four-thirty. Had a bit of quick sex with a labourer I picked up, some kind of roadmender. Then

Muted organ music.

the Chapel of Rest. It's a room, bare, white-washed. (*Referring to music.*) Just a tape. The coffin lid was propped up against the wall. It said 'Elsie Marie Orton. Aged 62 years.'

AUNT LUCY. They've got her age wrong. Elsie was 63. You tell them about that. Put in a complaint.

LEONIE. Auntie . . .

JOE. Why? It doesn't matter now.

AUNT LUCY. Well, we want it done right, don't we? It's what you pay for?

JOE (*to audience*). Mum's quite unrecognizable without her glasses. She looks old, fat and dead. (*Half-turning to the* UNDERTAKER.) They've made up her face.

UNDERTAKER. Would you say it wasn't discreet then, sir?

JOE. No, it seems alright to me.

UNDERTAKER. We try to give a life-like impression.

JOE (*to audience*). Which seems to be a contradiction in terms. Didn't sleep much. Awful bed. Damp and cold. House without Mum seems to have died . . .

December 30th

Got up early. Went downstairs and found Dad in the kitchen. He looks thin and old –

FATHER (*blindly*). Hallo?

JOE. – hardly more than a skeleton.

FATHER. Hallo.

JOE. Good morning.

FATHER. Hallo? Hallo? Who are you?

JOE. Joe. Joe. John. (*To audience.*) He couldn't remember I'd come back home last night.

FATHER. Do you know where my slippers are?

JOE (*to* FATHER). What do you mean, do I know?

FATHER. Have you seen my slippers?

JOE. Where are your slippers?

FATHER (*starting to feel around on the floor*). I can't find my slippers. I can't find my –

JOE. They're on your feet. Dad.

Father and son look at each other. Then JOE *turns to the audience.*

The dreadful, sickening wording on the wreaths: 'To a Dear Mum. At peace at last with little Tony, from Marilyn and Pete.' I was glad not to be involved. We all got into the cars. Aunt Lucy was getting furious because strict protocol wasn't being observed.

AUNT LUCY. They're all wrong. They shouldn't be with spouses. Just Immediate Circle should be in the First Car.

JOE (*to audience*). Several women were at their garden gates as the cortège passed. I noticed two old women weeping on each other's shoulders. It was a cold, bright morning. My mother's grave was a new one. Her last wish was to be buried with Tony, my nephew, but Marilyn and Pete refused to have the grave re-opened, Mother's last wish was ignored.

LEONIE. They've caused a lot of bad feeling all round. But she's hard. I can't understand her at all.

JOE. The coffin was lowered. The vicar said his piece. Father began to cry. And we walked back to the waiting cars. Immediately, a flock of women descended on the grave, picking over the wreaths and shaking their heads. We got back home at half past ten, for sandwiches and tea. The party got rather jolly.

AUNT LUCY. What's going to be done with your father?

JOE. We're taking him to the doctor's tomorrow.

AUNT LUCY. That's right. He wants a doctor. Ever since I can remember I've had a horror of abandoning old people. Well, there's nothing on my conscience. Poor, dear mother, bless her, lived with me for years. And she was no trouble. Your uncle and I had to change her bed clothes every day to prevent sores. She's been gone now for eight years, but if she came back tomorrow, I'd willingly have her.

JOE (*to his* FATHER *who is sitting, in a kind of reverie, looking very woebegone*). You okay, Dad?

FATHER. There was a time I thought of leaving her. Now and again. Used to give her my wage packet and she'd throw it back in me face. 'What am I supposed to do with this? Do wonders and shit miracles?' I don't know why I didn't leave her. You kids, I suppose.

AUNT LUCY (*to* FATHER, *as he goes*). Well, goodbye then. (FATHER *does not answer; so she turns to* JOE *and* LEONIE.) Elsie was very dear to me. I shan't come up here now she's gone. Goodbye. I hope you lot have a happier life than your Mum did.

LEONIE (*of* AUNT LUCY, *as she goes*). Silly moo.

LEONIE *and* JOE *kiss goodbye.*

'Bye.

JOE. Come down to London soon, eh? (*He parts from her and addresses the audience.*) And on the way back to the station, I picked up an Irishman. Pretty baggy. I wasn't going to bother but he had a place. It was an empty house, not derelict. He didn't live there. He rented it for sex. There was a table covered in grime. A huge mantlepiece with broken glass ornaments on it. He pulled the curtains which seemed unnecessary because the windows were so dirty. He had a white body, not in good condition. Going to fat. Very good sex, though. It was difficult to get in. A Catholic upbringing, I suppose. He wanted to fuck me when I'd finished. It seemed unfair to refuse since I'd fucked him. Afterwards, he showed me a photo of his fiancée.

January 2nd, 1967

(*To audience*). All day working on 'The Butler'. When Peter Willes rang, I told him about the funeral and the frenzied way my family behaved, he seemed shocked.

WILLES. My God, and I thought all your plays were fantasies.

JOE (*continuing to audience*). He suddenly caught a glimpse of the fact that I write the truth.

WILLES. I've booked us three tickets for tonight. What are we doing about dinner?

HALLIWELL (*taking the 'phone*). Joe and I shall have our sardines and golden syrup before we arrive. We shan't get there before seven-fifteen and I know that's much too early for you to dine.

WILLES. It's most unsociable of you not to have dinner after the show.

JOE. I don't want a meal so late.

HALLIWELL. Joe doesn't want to eat so late.

WILLES. Very well, but I shan't ask you again, though. I've never met such an extraordinary pair as you and Joe Orton. Why don't you get up an act and go busking?

He hangs up.

HALLIWELL. He's so Nineteen Thirties about dining out.

January 4th

JOE (*to audience*). Went down to see the *Loot* cast – since the funeral I had a new prop for Ken Cranham. Here, Ken, I thought you'd like the originals.

He hands him the false teeth.

CRANHAM. What?

JOE. Teeth.

CRANHAM. What?

JOE. My Mum's.

CRANHAM (*looking sick and handing them back*). God . . .

JOE. It's obvious you're not thinking of the events in the play in terms of reality. (*To* HALLIWELL.) Simon Ward shook like jelly when I gave them to him. (*He drops the teeth into a bedside glass of water.*) I don't understand it. I have great reverence for death but not for the dust of a corpse.

He drinks the water.

January 6th

(*To audience*). I helped Kenneth carry his collages down to an antique shop in Chelsea. The owner – Freddie – had plans for an ambitious exhibition.

FREDDIE. What have we here? (*He looks at them.*) Well, you've certainly got something here. (*He reads one.*) 'Rosencrantz was Jesus CHRIST?'?

HALLIWELL. Yes, you see it represents –

FREDDIE. I'll put them in this room.

JOE (*to audience*). An underground cavern.

FREDDIE. I'll make a show of it for you . . . I think they have to be dolled up a bit.

JOE. They want framing.

HALLIWELL. They want putting under glass. It'll bring out the colours.

FREDDIE. You want a nice framer. And what are you thinking of asking for them?

JOE. Let's leave that till they're framed and ready.

FREDDIE. Right you are. We'll leave it to fate then, shall we?

HALLIWELL. I'll have fifteen framed to start with.

FREDDIE. After all we don't know whether they're going to bite, do we?

January 11th

JOE (*to* HALLIWELL). Can I wear your flowery tie to the Awards Ceremony?

HALLIWELL. Just don't get it in the consommé.

JOE (*with very flowery, sixties tie*). Well? I think this is just right for the 'Oscar Wilde of the Welfare State'?

HALLIWELL. Perfect. Now you can walk down Piccadilly with a poppy *and* a lily.

JOE (*to audience*). And then on to the lunch at Quaglino's. Sheila greeted me with a conspiratorial whisper.

SHEILA. It's so grand!

JOE. It says on the board 'Mr. and Mrs. Orton'.

SHEILA. I'll be your wife for the afternoon.

JOE. How embarrassing if I had brought Kenneth. (*To the audience. Making acceptance speech and being handed the award.*) In the early days we used to give complimentary tickets to various organizations. We sent a few to Scotland Yard. They loved the play so much, they rang up asking for more tickets. Everyone else thinks *Loot* is a fantasy. Of course, the police know it's true. I hope to win another award in two years . . . That night, we watched a programme called *Accolade* about the awards. We invited Mr. and Mrs. Corden and Miss Boynes up to join us. It was a treat. (*Giving the menu to* MRS. CORDEN.) And this was the menu.

MRS. CORDEN. How lovely. It looks like a skilled printing job to me. But, of course, the actual luncheon isn't as good as Mr. Corden's firm's annual get-together dinner. It was at the Savoy and we had a sweet which was like straw. I have never, in my whole life, tasted anything so scruptious (*sic.*) That is the only word to describe it – scrumptious.

MISS BOYNES. I had a bite yesterday. From a businessman. Cheek! He offered three thousand.

JOE (*to audience*). She was talking about selling her flat.

BOYNES. Oh no! I'm not doing that. Not on your life, I'm not. The cheek!

MR. CORDEN (*examining the statuette*). Under this green baize is a bolt which bolts the actual object to the marble plinth. If you were to strip the baize away, you'd see the workmanship beneath.

JOE (*to audience*). Like turning round the Rokeby Venus to see

how the frame is made . . . The programme was a
disappointment: I appeared only briefly at the end with the
sound off and the captions going over my face. The sound came
on for the other winners. The whole had the effect of the man
with the bladder hitting the emperor in the face, just to remind
him that he wasn't a god. Went to bed very disgruntled.

He turns the TV off.

January 12th

The *Loot* hate-mail correspondence continues:

J.P.H. JOY. Dear Sir,
  On Saturday I went with my family to see *Loot* at your theatre,
  and feel compelled to express our disgust. As Christians, we
  were naturally dismayed to see the Roman Catholic Church
  abused, but even were I not a Christian I should have been
  ashamed to take my mother and sister to hear the
  accompanying filth. I am in consequence writing to the Lord
  Chamberlain. May I suggest that you should indicate to the
  public the immoral tone of the play. This would have spared us
  the annoyance of buying tickets for a play we felt forced to
  leave at the interval.
  Yours faithfully, J.P.H. Joy.

EDNA WELTHORPE. Dear J.P.H. Joy,
  It is wrong of me to write to you, I'm sure. Your letter was
  passed to me for filing and I do hope you respect my confidence
  in this. Your letter has received the most respectful attention
  here – for you are not alone in disliking the play *Loot*. I myself
  consider it to be the most loathsome play in London at the
  present moment. 'Bestial' is how I described it the other day.
  When I tell you that in the second act (which you had the good
  fortune to miss) there was a discussion upon the raping of
  children with Mars bars with other filthy details of a sexual and
  psychopathic nature I'm sure you'll pardon my writing. Please,
  as a fellow Christian, let me applaud your design in writing to
  the Lord Chamberlain. I myself am trying to contact my MP at
  the moment. This truly horrible play shouldn't contaminate our
  streets. I am also seeking, in a solo capacity, to arrange a
  meeting with the Lord Chamberlain to protest against plays in
  general and this travesty of the free society, *Loot*, in particular.

I wonder if you'd like to be included in our mission?
Yours, in great sympathy, Edna Welthorpe, Mrs.

JOE (*referring to* EDNA). I like that one. I wrote it.

HALLIWELL. Yes, but what if J.P.H. Joy writes back to Edna
and says she does want to go and see the Lord Chamberlain?

JOE (*not rising to his pedantry*). No one's walked out since the day
the award was announced. Now they've been told they can
enjoy it, they do.

HALLIWELL. I thought it was rather an intelligent audience last
night.

JOE. I don't give a fuck about their intelligence. How many of
them were there?

HALLIWELL. Corrupted already?

JOE. Any intelligent person should have seen the play weeks ago.
All I'm interested in now is their money.

EDNA WELTHORPE. May I add my thoughts on the subject of
those 'much-talked-of' awards?

JOE (*to audience*). *Plays and Players* have printed Edna's latest!

EDNA. I agree that no-one should seriously nominate as Play of
the Year a piece of indecent tomfoolery like *Loot*. Drama should
be uplifting. The plays of Joe Orton have a most unpleasant
effect on me. I was plunged into the dumps for weeks after
seeing his *Entertaining Mr. Sloane*. I saw *Loot* with my young
niece; we both fled from the theatre in horror and amazement
long before the end. I could see no humour in it. Yet it is widely
advertised as a rib-tickler. Surely this is wrong? These plays do
nothing but harm to our image abroad, presenting us as the
slaves of sensation and unnatural practice.
Yours, Edna Welthorpe, Mrs.

The 'phone starts ringing. JOE *ignores it, eventually* HALLIWELL
is forced to answer it.

HALLIWELL. Hallo.

SHENSON. Can I speak with Mr. Orton, please?

HALLIWELL. Whom shall I say is calling?

SHENSON. Walter Shenson.

HALLIWELL (*to* JOE). For you.

JOE (*to* HALLIWELL, *trying to be nice*). For me? (*He puts the receiver to his ear.*) Hello?

SHENSON. Hello, Joe, you don't know me but I am producing another film for the Beatles, and I've got this script. It isn't quite good enough. Would you like to see it with a view to working on the screenplay.

JOE (*covering 'phone*). I was very impressed but put on a nonchalant manner. (*Into 'phone.*) Well, I'm frightfully up to my eyes in it at the moment, Walter. I am writing my third play.

SHENSON. I'd certainly love you to have a look. I've discussed it with the boys. I mean I mentioned your name to them. They've heard of you. They didn't react too much, I must say. But I believe I can persuade them.

JOE. Well . . . (*Then hurriedly.*) Send the script over. (*He turns to* HALLIWELL, *full of excitement.*) The Beatles, they want me to –

HALLIWELL. Yes, I heard.

JOE. I'll use my old bag of tricks from 'Sloane' and *Loot*. It doesn't matter if I repeat myself. Nobody who sees the film will have ever been in a theatre. I think I'll rehabilitate the plot of *The Silver Bucket*. Where is it?

He looks for the script and finds it.

HALLIWELL (*bristling*). I wrote that.

JOE. We did. Our first novel? . . . 1953, wasn't it?

HALLIWELL. You didn't write, you typed.

Pause.

JOE. Well, I write now.

HALLIWELL. And I can't. I don't understand it.

JOE. I grew up.

HALLIWELL. And I grew old.

JOE. Don't start.

HALLIWELL. You're quite a different person, you know, since you've had your success. Not a thought for my feelings. You couldn't even spell. To you, a plot was a grave, for God's sake. *The Silver Bucket's* just as much mine as yours.

JOE. OK, you sell it to the Beatles. (*He hands HALLIWELL the manuscript. HALLIWELL goes and flings it in the bin. JOE watches and then retrieves the manuscript, sits at the desk and starts work on it. HALLIWELL watches him, and then defiantly turns the TV on, loud. After a pause, to the audience.*) So, watched an old film called *My Favourite Brunette*, with Bob Hope. This had sentimental overtones for me. It was at this picture, some time in the late Forties, that I was first interfered with. A man took me into the lavatory of the Odeon and gave me a wank. I relived the happy moments as we watched. I remember coming down his mac. I must've been fourteen.

January 16th

(*To audience*). Saw Mrs. Corden today, in her outfit for the firm's annual get-together.

MRS. CORDEN. It came from Africa the material. All the way from Africa.

JOE (*to audience*). I wasn't too surprised. She looked like a fucking Hottentot in it . . . And then Miss Boynes, full of the holiday spirit!

MISS BOYNES. The Cordens are the filthiest people I've ever met. I had to do Mrs. Corden's hair for her appearance at the Savoy. And you know I can't stand touching other people's hair. I did it for the goodwill. But really, you know, she looked a sight. I had a little laugh to myself as she drove off.

January 25th

SHENSON. So, you'll be hearing from either Brian or Paul in the near future. So don't be surprised if a Beatle rings you up.

JOE. It'll be like having St. Michael or God on the line.

SHENSON. There's no need to worry, Joe. I can say, from my heart, that the boys are most respectful of talent. I mean, most respectful of anyone they feel has talent. I can really say that, Joe.

JOE (*to audience*). Wandering about the Holloway Road, met a middle-aged man. Not very attractive.

MIDDLE-AGED MAN. You don't want it stuck up your arse, do you?

JOE (*to* MAN). I'm not keen.

MIDDLE-AGED MAN. And you're not going to suck me off, are you?

JOE. No.

MIDDLE-AGED MAN. You just want to shoot your gun, like me. You can pick up a queer in that toilet. They've got cars. And houses. I've fucked their arses in their rooms. Expect you have too.

JOE (*to audience*). Went to see Paul McCartney instead. An old man answered the door. (*To* BUTLER.) I've come to see The Beatles.

BUTLER. One moment, sir.

JOE (*to audience*). I suddenly realised the man was The Butler. I've never seen one before.

BUTLER (*announcing*). Mr. Joseph Orton.

JOE. Everybody stood up. Even Paul McCartney.

McCARTNEY. The only thing I get from the theatre is a sore arse. I liked *Loot*, though. I'd've liked a bit more.

JOE (*to* McCARTNEY). Compared to the pop scene the theatre is square, man. The theatre started going downhill when Queen Victoria knighted Henry Irving. Too fucking respectable. But listen, Paul, I'd like to do the film. There's only one thing we've got to fix up.

McCARTNEY. You mean the bread?

JOE. Yes. (*To* HALLIWELL.) Whether I do it or not is a matter of indifference to me.

HALLIWELL. You should be asking for fifteen thousand and a percentage.

JOE. And if they won't pay me ten, they can fuck themselves.

A silence.

HALLIWELL (*looking at* JOE's *new socks*). How much did you pay for these?

JOE. Nineteen and six. I bought six pairs.

HALLIWELL. That's outrageous. You can get them for seven and six in the market, and better quality.

JOE. I can afford it.

Another niggly silence.

HALLIWELL. Are you going to wear your blue suit this summer?

JOE. No.

HALLIWELL. Then why did you have the trousers altered? If you hadn't had them altered I could've worn them.

JOE. But if you could wear them, they wouldn't have fitted me. That's why I had them altered.

HALLIWELL. And now they don't fit me.

JOE. No. But if they'd've fitted you, they wouldn't've fitted me. And as they didn't fit me, I had them altered. And now I've had them altered, they don't fit you.

February 6th

(*To audience*). Went to Brian Epstein's office to talk about *Up Against It*, as I've decided to call my screenplay. They made me wait. (*He flicks idly through a magazine.*) All the newspapers are quite hysterical about Sir Francis Chichester, an old man who sailed round the Horn because he couldn't get one of his own.

BROWN (*entering hastily*). Mr. Orton? I'm Peter Brown, Mr. Epstein's personal assistant. I'm afraid there's been a most awful mix-up. And all the Boys' appointments have been put back an hour and a half.

JOE (*chilly*). Well, what should I do? Come back at six?

BROWN. Could we make another appointment?

JOE. What guarantee is there you won't break that? I think you'd better find yourself another writer.

BROWN. I'll see what I can do. (*He goes.*)

JOE (*to audience as* EPSTEIN *enters*). I expected Epstein to be florid, Jewish, dark-haired and over-bearing. Instead, I was face to face with a mousey, slight, young man –

EPSTEIN. Could you meet me and The Boys for dinner tonight?

JOE (*continuing*). – with a suburban accent.

EPSTEIN. We do want to have the pleasure of your company.

JOE. I've got another engagement.

EPSTEIN. Could I send a car for you after that engagement?

JOE. Yeah, I suppose, OK. (*To audience.*) After a lot of polite flim-flammery, I left, almost tripping over the carpet and crashing into the secretary who gave a squeal of surprise as I stumbled past her. (*She does so.*) This I never mention when re-telling the story. I always end on a note of hurt dignity.

February 9th

JOE. Kenneth and I went down in the bus to the Libyan Embassy for visas.

MAN. It's sevenpence to where I'm going, my dear. I remember when it was two pence.

WOMAN. Do you really?

MAN. You don't mind me speaking to you without your permission, do you?

WOMAN. No.

MAN. Thank you. I usually travel by underground. I'm a railway official. We travel free of charge. As I expect you've read. (*Pause.*) When I get home my four-footed friend will run to greet me . . . my dog.

JOE (*to audience*). As though she might imagine he meant his donkey.

HALLIWELL (*as they walk away, in anger*). Come back tomorrow! I always knew we shouldn't try to go to a country with visas!

JOE. Peter says they queue up outside your door in Libya!

HALLIWELL. I don't believe in going where I'm not wanted.

JOE (*to* HALLIWELL). Why should they want me?

HALLIWELL (*in quite a rage by now*). I can't get the photographs changed in time! It's just not possible. . . .

JOE. Wait and see if that's what they want. They may just wish to check you're not your brother.

February 11th

(*To audience*). Meeting with Shenson about the Beatles script.

SHENSON. Joe, I'm concerned to impress upon you the immensity of the Boys' popularity.

JOE. Of course.

The action now splits into two. JOE *and* SHENSON *continue their conversation, but it is interspliced with* HALLIWELL *talking to* MISS BOYNES.

HALLIWELL. How are Sweep, Jen-Jen?

BOYNES. I'm just changing their cage. You wouldn't care to give me a hand, would you?

HALLIWELL. You have but to ask, Doris.

SHENSON. They shouldn't do anything in the film that would reflect badly on them.

JOE. . . . No.

BOYNES. You've got such a nice manner, Kenneth. You're well spoken. You don't take advantage of the 'phone. You're a gentleman.

HALLIWELL *just smiles.*

SHENSON. You see, The Boys must always be on their best behaviour.

JOE. Yes. I'm a great fan of the Beatles.

HALLIWELL. John's writing a film for the Beatles. And *Loot*'s been sold to the movies.

BOYNES. It's your year.

HALLIWELL. His year.

BOYNES (*ingenuously*). You've got a lovely voice, Kenneth.

SHENSON. The kids will all imitate whatever the Boys do.

JOE (*to audience*). I hadn't the heart to tell him that the Boys, in my screenplay, have been caught 'in flagrante', become involved in dubious political activity, dressed as women, committed murder, adultery and end up in prison. (*Pause.*) And the script isn't finished yet.

SHENSON. I'm glad we're on the same wavelength here, Joe.

BOYNES. You shouldn't stay at home so much. You'll get depressed.

HALLIWELL. I am depressed.

SHENSON. Our legal people drag their butts, Joe. But you should have your contract in the next couple of days.

JOE. Right.

They shake hands.

HALLIWELL. I have a history of depression.

JOE (*to audience*). But I decided to say nothing.

HALLIWELL. The pills don't help.

JOE (*to audience*). Anyway, I've almost finished it.

BOYNES. A job would keep you busy. Get you out of the house.

JOE (*to audience*). I'm going up.

HALLIWELL. I don't want a job.

JOE (*to audience*). Up.

HALLIWELL. I like being at home.

JOE (*to audience*). Up!

February 13th

JOE (*to audience*). We went to see the collages framed for the exhibition.

FREDDIE. I think they're going to bite, but I can't hang this one.

He hands it back.

HALLIWELL. 'Cosy Couples'? Why not?

FREDDIE. Some of my friends have warned me that I could be liable to prosecution.

JOE. Nervous twit. Like all the middle-classes. Too nervous to live.

HALLIWELL (*to* ORTON, *as he hangs 'Cosy Couples' in the flat*).
Anyway, who's going to want to go and see pictures stuck away
at the wrong end of King's Road?

JOE. It's going to be OK. (*To audience*.) It would be nice if he
could sell some.

February 24th

(*To audience*). Libya! Two weeks of hashish and bum!

HALLIWELL. What extraordinary people to be at Gatwick at
this time in the morning. They really shouldn't allow this kind
of riff-raff in the airport at all. I don't want a lot of people in
the airport I'm leaving from. It's spoiling everything. (*Pause*.) I
had a dream last night that we went to get our tickets and the
plane was full.

JOE. I wonder you don't start chewing leaves like the Delphic
Oracle. (*To audience*.) At Idris Airport.

AIRPORT LIBYAN. You no have reservation? Everywhere
always is booked.

HALLIWELL *looks pole-axed*, JOE *notices this*.

Maybe you try Libya Palace. And if no get in there, go to
Delmahari.

JOE. The Libya Palace was full.

HALLIWELL. I'm not staying here, you know that, don't you.

JOE. The Delmahari was full.

HALLIWELL. I can tell already it's dreadul.

JOE. The desk clerk suggested a ship.

HALLIWELL. A ship! We'll find ourselves in Saudi Arabia
branded as slaves.

LIBYAN CLERK. Ship very good hotel. Hot and cold in all
room.

JOE. *The Carina* was a second, third class ex-German cruise ship.

LIBYAN MANAGER. We have only double room. Eight pound
ten.

JOE. A week?

LIBYAN MANAGER. A night.

JOE. For two?

LIBYAN MANAGER. For one.

JOE. We'll take it.

HALLIWELL (*they squeeze, with difficulty, into the tiny cabin.*) Oh my God! Look what a mess you've got us in now. Dumped on a ship in the middle of some wretched fascist state. I'm going to faint.

JOE. Pull yourself together. There's no need to behave badly.

HALLIWELL. I warned you what it would be like. No travel agency does Libya. And I'm not surprised. This is probably a brothel.

JOE (*to audience*). Our room was the size of a generous linen cupboard.

HALLIWELL. We could stay at the Hilton for this price.

JOE (*to* HALLIWELL). We must make the best of it. Go and have a shower. It's good for the nerves.

HALLIWELL. Fuck the shower. I must have a glass of water. Where's the Alka-Seltzer?

JOE. Alka-Seltzer isn't sold as a protective against typhoid.

HALLIWELL. No, but it makes the water taste better. Sleep will be impossible tonight.

JOE (*to audience*). It was. So the next day we flew back to London. (*To* WILLES.) Not a sign of a cock – except my own and that only glimpsed briefly in a cracked mirror. Altogether it was like a balmy night in Birkenhead.

NICHOLA. It'll be good for publicity.

WILLES. You can write it off as collecting 'local colour'. And Kenneth – simply claim he's your 'personal assistant'.

HALLIWELL *takes umbrage and walks away. An embarrassed moment.*

WILLES. Sorry, Joe . . .

JOE. Still, it was only about a hundred pounds.

WILLES. For both of you?

JOE. Kenneth was another hundred.

WILLES. It's disgraceful. The problems of the rich!

JOE. There was no problem. I hated it and came back. You can do that when you're rich.

WILLES. This has been so upsetting. I shall have to go and have a cup of coffee with my mother.

He goes.

NICHOLA. You should have asked to be taken to a brothel. You should have gone to a brothel and declared 'If any of you gentlemen fancies me, I'm only too ready to oblige!'

JOE. Sex was of secondary importance.

March 9th

HALLIWELL. Now I've got a pain in my chest. It's from the Benzyle Benzoate I put on my chest for my spots.

JOE. Don't be silly. A dab of ointment can't cause heart palpitations. See a doctor.

HALLIWELL. I saw a doctor two weeks ago, don't you remember? I don't trust him.

JOE. Why not?

HALLIWELL. He said I was imagining it. 'It's because your mother died when you were eleven. You are imagining this heart condition out of guilt.'

JOE. Whatever are you guilty about?

HALLIWELL. I don't know, the pain is real.

JOE. Take some tranquilizers –

HALLIWELL. The exhibition's a wash-out. No-one's buying.

JOE. At least they cut down the yapping.

HALLIWELL. You're turning into a real bully, do you know that? You better be careful. You'll get your just deserts.

JOE (*to audience*). Went to sleep.

March 11th

Doorbell. HALLIWELL, *on his own now, panics.*

WILLIAMS. Hullo.

HALLIWELL. Yes? . . . Joe's not here.

WILLIAMS. Well, I'll come and visit you . . . Aren't you going to ask me in?

HALLIWELL. But he's not here. You don't want to see me.

WILLIAMS. Nonsense, I'd love to see you. Your inferiority is preposterous. Of course I want to see you. And I can smell something cooking.

HALLIWELL. Oh, it's a bit of haddock I'm doing for him.

WILLIAMS. I love haddock.

HALLIWELL. There's only enough for two.

WILLIAMS. Rubbish. Split the two bits and put an egg on top. We'll all have it.

JOE (*entering*). Ken!

WILLIAMS. Joe.

JOE. Sit down. (*They do so.*) What are you doing here?

WILLIAMS (*dropping the façade*). Loose end, really. This left-over life of mine.

HALLIWELL. I know how you feel.

WILLIAMS. I can't stand being alone. I can't abide it. You always seem to find friends.

JOE. Yes . . . yesterday, I saw this bloke outside the lav on Talbot Road.

WILLIAMS (*gleeful*). Filth! Filth!!

JOE. We'd been eyeing each other warily. Finally, I went over to him and he asks 'You gotta place we can go?' I told him I lived with someone and it wasn't convenient. 'I often get picked up by queers round here,' he said. 'Some of them have very nice places. I've had as much as thirty bob. They're not effeminate either. You'd never dream they were queer. Not from the look of them. But I can always tell – they've ALL got Judy Garland LPs. That's the big giveaway.'

WILLIAMS. Marvellous! You really get the flavour.

JOE. Yes. I've started a diary. And you're in it.

WILLIAMS. Oh yes?

HALLIWELL. Pepys put all his references to sexual matters in code.

WILLIAMS. So no one would know.

JOE (*looking straight at* HALLIWELL). I don't care who knows. There isn't a secret in Western Civilization worth keeping.

HALLIWELL (*changing the subject and referring to the newspaper he has been reading*). There's a theatre group in America, The Living Theatre, that encourages orgies on the stage. Complete sexual licence.

JOE. It's the only way to smash the wretched civilization.

HALLIWELL. Like the Albighensian Heresy.

WILLIAMS (to JOE). Eleventh Century.

JOE. Yes. Much more fucking and they'll be screaming hysterics in next to no time. I must remember to hot up *What the Butler Saw* when I rewrite.

March 18th

HALLIWELL. I hope I die of heart disease! I'd like to see you manage then.

JOE (*to audience*). Kenneth still suffering with 'His Chest'.

HALLIWELL. This is Strindberg. We're living it!

March 28th

JOE. Long walk through Regent's Park. Sunshine and the first ghastliness of Spring. Found the café was partially open and bought an orangeade and a Coca-Cola. Sat in the blazing light and noticed how hideous the bright sunshine made everyone appear – myself included. Like blanched and unsavoury apes.

April 3rd

(*To audience*). Kenneth has now decided what is wrong with him.

HALLIWELL. It's not my heart, it's my liver.

JOE (*to audience*). He isn't eating. Just sipping milk. Most tiresome, if he decides to go on hunger strike. I shall now get my own meals. This doesn't worry me particularly, except that it does mean we're starting to live quite separate lives.

Pause. He looks at HALLIWELL.

(*To* HALLIWELL). You look like a zombie.

HALLIWELL. So I should, I lead the life of a zombie.

JOE. I think it's bad we live in each other's pockets twenty-four hours a day, three hundred and sixty-five days a year. Living together in one tiny room. When I'm out you do nothing, meet nobody.

HALLIWELL. I need an affair with someone. You're no good. You're only interested in physical sex, not love. Your attitude to sensitive people is Victorian. Basically it's Dr. Arnold: 'Get out on the playing fields, you won't be sensitive then.'

JOE. All you need is some field of interest outside me. Where you can meet people away from me.

Meanwhile, HALLIWELL *gets up, crosses to where the exhibition collages are, collects them and brings them back, while* FREDDIE *says.*

FREDDIE. Sorry, Kenneth, they didn't seem to bite.

HALLIWELL. I'll kill myself. I will kill myself, I'll commit suicide, you'll learn then, won't you. What will you be like without me!

Short pause. Then HALLIWELL *seizes the diary and flings it down.*

I'm disgusted by all this immorality. Homosexuals disgust me!

JOE. I won't try to fathom that one out.

HALLIWELL (*starting to shout and bang walls*). I'm not going to Morocco for a holiday. I'm going to kill myself. I've led a dreadful, unhappy life. I'm pathetic. I can't go on suffering like this . . . All those years of work. What do I have to show for it?

JOE. We share everything.

HALLIWELL. Everything except success.

JOE. I do the work.

HALLIWELL. You knew nothing when you met me. You were half-baked. I showed you what to wear, what to read, how to speak and think. Everything you write comes out of what I did.

JOE. What am I supposed to do? Everybody we know knows how important you are. I tell them.

HALLIWELL. Fuck everybody we know. They only see the public Joe Orton. This is a collaboration. Why don't you admit it?

JOE. C'mon.

JOE *tries to touch* HALLIWELL.

HALLIWELL. Get off . . . I've wasted my life.

JOE. Don't be silly.

HALLIWELL. I'm as bright as you. I've worked as hard. Read as much. And as for wit – God knows there are enough of my lines in your plays. But does anybody know my name? All I have is the dedication page in 'Sloane'. And Page Three of your income tax return where I'm billed as 'Personal Assistant'. I'm forty-one. Bald! (*At which point he rips off his wig, revealing total baldness.*) The sum total of my accomplishments thus far, in what I laughingly call my life, is as a tax write-off!

JOE. What do you want?

HALLIWELL. I want some acknowledgement. I want to be included. Not just to make up a dinner, not just as the friend, 'The Difficult Friend' – yes, I know that's how you all see me – I want to be part of your fame. After all, I made you. Without me, you couldn't write the way you do.

JOE. Oh, please. I learned to write in prison. The only time I've been away from you.

HALLIWELL (*only momentarily beaten*). You wouldn't even have been in prison if I hadn't written the letter that got us nicked for the library books. Anyway, that's not the point. I read what you told that man from the magazine – 'I like Lucian and the classical writers. I suppose that's what gives my writing a difference. An old-fashioned classical education which I never received but gave myself.' I gave you that education. The difference in your writing is ME.

JOE. So what are the posters supposed to read 'Written by Joe Orton. Education by Kenneth Halliwell'?

HALLIWELL. I don't know. Something . . . something . . .

JOE. What?

HALLIWELL. Something to show I was there. I helped.

JOE. But you got what you wanted.

HALLIWELL. What was that, pray?

JOE. A friend.

HALLIWELL. That's what I'm asking you to be now . . . A friend.

JOE. You don't want a friend. You want a Fairy Godmother.

A pause. Then, HALLIWELL *leaps at* JOE *and starts pumelling him about the head, forcing him down onto the bed. They struggle for a moment, until* JOE *gets control of* HALLIWELL. *They remain locked in a wrestlers' embrace, as* HALLIWELL *starts to sob, and say,*

HALLIWELL. Help me . . . Help me . . . Help me . . .

JOE *rests his head on* HALLIWELL.

The lights slowly fade.

ACT TWO

JOE (*to audience*). Later, I popped into a little pissoir on the Holloway Road. It was dark – someone had stolen the bulb. There were three figures pissing. I had a piss. As my eyes got used to the gloom, I saw that one of the figures was worth having – a labouring type, big, with cropped hair. Another man entered and the man next to the labouring type moved away, not out of the place altogether, but back against the wall. The new man had a pee and left and before the man against wall could return to his place, I nipped in there sharpish and stood next to the labourer. I put my hand down and felt his cock, he immediately started to play with mine. The youngish man with fair hair standing next to the wall went into the vacant place. I unbuttoned the top of my jeans to allow the labourer free rein. The man next to me began to feel my bum. At this point a fifth man entered. Nobody moved. It was dark. Just a little light spilled into the place, not enough to see immediately. But the fifth man very quickly flashed his cock and so the man next to me returned to my side, lifting up my coat and shoving his hand down the back of my trousers. A sixth man came into the pissoir. We all looked. After an interval (during which the fifth man watched me feel the labourer, the labourer stroked my cock, and the man beside me pulled my jeans down still further), I noticed that the sixth man was kneeling down beside the youngish man with fair hair and sucking his cock. A seventh man came in, but by now nobody cared. The number of people in the place was so large that arrests would be quite impossible. The little pissoir under the bridge had become the scene of a frenzied homosexual saturnalia. And no more than two feet away the citizens of Holloway moved about their ordinary business.

I caught the bus home.

The lights come up revealing HALLIWELL *and* WILLIAMS *also in the bedsitter.*

HALLIWELL. It sounds as though eightpence and a bus down the Holloway Road was more interesting than two hundred pounds and a plane to Tripoli.

WILLIAMS. I hope you'll get in touch with Clive and Tom,

they'll introduce you to the Holloway Set.

JOE. Clive's the one works on the telephones, isn't he?

WILLIAMS. That's him. A dish. He'll love the filthy talk. Loves all the filth, dear.

HALLIWELL. Sounds a waste of spunk to me.

JOE. So who are the Holloway Set?

WILLIAMS. Well, this doctor in Holloway, a queen but good natured, has bought this house and stocked it with boys. They're all working lads, all from borstal. And she's allotted them their various tasks. One is responsible for the plumbing, another for electricity, she's even got a boy responsible for the goldfish. And if one neglects his task, she calls him in to the surgery, wags her finger and says: 'What is your excuse?', and the lad might say 'Well, I had the trade in and forgot.' 'Forgot!' this queen will say, 'Forgot? Had the trade in and forgot? You've no right to have the trade until you've fed the fucking goldfish!'

HALLIWELL. I don't see the point of sex with your inferiors.

JOE. You would if you got lucky.

HALLIWELL. I'm never lucky. You, however, were born with a horsehoe up your arse.

JOE. Luck comes to the prepared cock.

WILLIAMS (*trying to defuse the rising tension*). Remember George Johnson, you know, who used to play the violin at the Palm Court? Well, George was staying in Bristol in terrible digs. He'd been having trade back and finally his landlady said 'Mister Johnson, you've been bringing people back, haven't you? It's got to stop.' So Johnson stopped. But on his last night in Bristol he met a sailor and thought 'Well, fuck it, I'm having this.' So he took the sailor back to his room, but – so that the landlady would only hear one set of feet, he gave the/sailor a piggy-back up the stairs. As he passed the landlady's room, carrying the sailor, the landlady opened her door and looked out. She pursed her lips and said: 'Bringing back cripples now, are you?'

They laugh.

(*As he stands to leave*). I'm very fond of you, Joe, I'm so glad you're coming on my programme.

JOE. For me, TV is virgin territory.

WILLIAMS. Well, in your case, Joe, 'virgin' is an honorary title.

He goes.

JOE (*addressing the audience*). So we met Clive and Tom for a drink a week later. Tom was about thirty, nice, but middle-class. I hoped a bit of sex with Tom might put an end to Kenneth's moods. (*To* HALLIWELL.) I gave them our telephone number.

HALLIWELL. You should have asked for theirs . . . Which one did you like?

JOE. Clive, of course.

HALLIWELL. To my mind, Tom was infinitely preferable – for sex and company. Shall we ask them around for a meal?

JOE. Why not? Faint heart never won fair maiden.

April 25th

JOE (*to audience*). We went to visit Mrs. Corden in hospital. She'd spilled a cup of tea in her lap and scalded herself.

MRS. CORDEN. My vagina has come up the size of a football. Matron said to me that in all her years of medical expertise she'd never seen nothing like it. But I've no complaints about the treatment. I've been given top-class penicillin.

JOE (*to audience*). Unpleasant day. Constant rowing over small things. Went for a walk to Golders Hill to see the animals.

HALLIWELL. Look at those miniature deer.

JOE (*withering*). Horrible rat-like creatures.

HALLIWELL. You have no interest in nature. I don't understand you, you'd be content to strut up and down the Pentonville Road until your balls drop off. I'm fed up to the back teeth with your constant moaning. You're the difficult one to live with. Everybody says so.

JOE. Who?

HALLIWELL. Oh, everybody . . . Peter Willes, Sheila

Ballantine, Kenneth Williams. They all know that I'm the easy going one.

JOE. You're getting to be a fucking 'mater dolorosa', aren't you?

HALLIWELL. You know I'm taking tablets to calm me down, and you're working overtime to counteract the effect, aren't you?

JOE (*ignoring him, and absorbed in his own concerns*). Epstein is an amateur and a fool.

HALLIWELL. I don't want to talk about the screenplay any more.

JOE. He isn't equipped to judge the quality of the script. Probably he will never say yes. Equally he hasn't the courage to say no.

HALLIWELL. I refuse to utter one more syllable on the Fab fucking Four.

JOE. I shall give the script to Oscar. He likes it. He'd probably do it better anyway. I just don't understand why they bother to commission a script and then wait until it's taken away from them.

HALLIWELL. Maybe they don't like it.

JOE. You think?

HALLIWELL. Don't ask me. You're the professional writer.

JOE (*to audience*). When we got home, Kenneth watched television, so I wrote a letter.

HALLIWELL *turns on the television, it is 'Juke Box Jury'*.

EDNA WELTHORPE. Dear Mr. Williams,
I must take up cudgels with you over your recent appearance on *Juke Box Jury*. I regretted many of your remarks which, in my opinion, were quite uncalled-for and tasteless in the extreme. Especially offensive to me as a nursing mother was your attack on infants and their ways. My own baby, born recently, cried throughout the programme. Which, I feel, more than proves my point.
More serious was your veiled threat to wear plastic earrings. This greatly disturbed me and my whole family. We were not alone in our fright. The usually irrepressible 'Millie' Martin seemed quite put out by your vile decision to flout convention.

For the rest of the evening – long after you had left our screen –
the idea was discussed among my family circle.

I cannot condemn too strongly the whole sorry business, made
especially more deplorable for me as I thoroughly enjoyed many
of the records which found no favour with you. Saturday Night
viewers must be protected from people like you.

Yours faithfully,

Edna Welthorpe (Mrs.)

JOE. I finally got through to Clive and Tom. Their 'phone's been
out of order. I invited them round. But Tom's away. I've asked
Clive to *Loot*.

HALLIWELL. What do you want to do that for? It means
having sex at midnight. If Tom's away, you could've gone up
there and had sex any time of the evening.

JOE. I can't just ring up and suggest coming over for sex. I mean,
even for me that's a bit crude. I've got to wrap it up a bit.

HALLIWELL. Don't know why you bother. He's dead behind
the eyes, that one.

JOE. It's not his eyes I'm interested in.

HALLIWELL. Your definition of a man: a life support system
for a penis.

JOE. As a definition, it's better than most. And besides, I'm not
interested in futile 'relationships'. Those I can have with my
equals.

And JOE *goes on typing the letter. The television starts playing the
'Call My Bluff' theme.*

EDNA WELTHORPE. Dear Mr. Williams,

Bravo for your splendid performance in the panel game *What's
My Bluff* (Friday). I was enthralled at your masterful control of
what could, and I'm sure on many occasions was, a tense and
difficult situation.

The way you held your team was brilliant. I'm sure Miss
Maxine Audrey and Mr. Joe Horton must've taken some
handling. But you showed you were a past-master of the art of
diplomacy. Let us see more of you on television in the future!
And here's power to your elbow.

Yours sincerely,

Edna Welthorpe (Mrs.)

May 5th

JOE (*to audience*). Kenneth Halliwell and I had a long talk about our relationship. He threatens, or rather keeps saying, he'll kill himself.

HALLIWELL (*very uptight*). I will.

JOE. Ken.

HALLIWELL. When I'm dead, you'll learn then. What'll you do without me?

JOE. All you need to cheer yourself up is a steady regimen of boys, beach and bum. We'll be back in Tangiers on Monday.

HALLIWELL. What I need is love. You don't love me the way I love you. That's my trouble. You love your trade.

JOE *raises an eyebrow at this unintended innuendo.*

Your WRITING. You love your public.

JOE. Ken . . .

HALLIWELL. But you don't love me. I'll kill myself if you leave me.

JOE. I didn't say I'd leave you –

HALLIWELL. I've got enough Nembutals. I'll take an overdose. Look at me, Joe, I'm not kidding.

JOE. I didn't say I'd leave you. I said I needed some space apart from you. We can't go on like this. You exhaust me. I can't write.

HALLIWELL. And you've exhausted me. I can't live. What have I got? Evil to look back on, nothing to look forward to, and pain in the present.

JOE. When you're in a moth, there's no reasoning with you.

HALLIWELL. 'You can't be rational in an irrational world. It isn't rational.' To quote myself from one of your plays. Knowing you, my suicide'd probably be just another play for you. Might as well, you've used everything else.

JOE. Shut up, that's unfair.

HALLIWELL. Who's unfair?

JOE. If you do top yourself, I know what I'll call the play.

HALLIWELL. Titles are not your forte. You'll never be able to write without me.

JOE. 'Sulking for Keeps'.

HALLIWELL *advances threateningly on* JOE. *The front door bell rings.*

HALLIWELL. Jesus. Clive and Tom.

HALLIWELL, *in panic, puts his wig on, while* JOE *speaks.*

May 6th

JOE (*to audience*). Clive and I definitely hit it off, but Kenneth was determined not to show any interest.

HALLIWELL. You'll have to face up to the world one day.

JOE. You are driving me crazy.

HALLIWELL. You're driving me crazy. Clive and Tom treated me like shit. They ignored me. They shut me out. I won't be treated like this.

JOE. All they did was agree with me.

HALLIWELL. You had tea, they had tea. You had jam tarts, they had jam tarts, you admired –

JOE. Surely you expected this.

HALLIWELL (*crying*). I expected to be treated with a little respect. All that typical queer talk. I've heard it all before.

JOE. All I wanted was a bit of a knock with Clive. I wasn't interested in Tom. He was for you. As it is, it looks like Hell Hath No Fury.

HALLIWELL. I sometimes think I'm against all you stand for. Well, I'll be gone soon.

JOE. I won't have you monopolizing the agony market.

HALLIWELL. If you have Clive AND Tom, you can say goodbye to me.

May 7th

JOE (*to audience*). Tea with the neighbours.

MR. AND MRS. CORDEN, MISS BOYNES, JOE *and*

HALLIWELL *congregate, each holding a tea cup.*

MISS BOYNES. Well, I've sold my flat. For two thousand, seven hundred and fifty pounds. Excluding taxes. Whatever they may be.

MRS. CORDEN. My Ernest knows all there is to know about taxes. Don't you, Ernest?

MR. CORDEN. Yeah, 'ere's a good one. You want to ring for a taxi. Go to the West End. Note carefully the fare and, when you come home, double it. And if anybody says anything, swear blind that you came home by taxi when, in reality, you came home by bus. See, there are many fiddles the ordinary person will not take the trouble to learn.

MRS. CORDEN. That's quite right. Mr. Corden works for a firm of accountants.

MISS BOYNES. He's the caretaker!

An embarrassed silence.

HALLIWELL. Are you thinking of getting a dog when you move to your new bungalow, Doris?

MISS BOYNES. Well, there's many factors, Kenneth. There's my new Axminsters to think of.

She goes.

MRS. CORDEN. She's so houseproud. The most beaujolais woman I've ever known.

JOE *and* HALLIWELL *laugh, she thinks in agreement.*

MRS. CORDEN. It's the truth, isn't it? I speak as I find.

The party breaks up.

JOE (*to audience*). But when I got back into the flat:

HALLIWELL *now daubs the words 'Joe Orton is a spineless twat' over the walls of the room. When he finishes, he sits sulkily on the bed and* JOE *faces the audience and says.*

Well, at least he's overcome his writer's block. But he had also been to the doctor and got four hundred valium. Later, we took two each and had an amazing sex session.

HALLIWELL (*painfully*). You can fuck me if you want to.

JOE. I'm not sure what the block is. I can fuck other people perfectly well. But I still can't fuck you.

May 8th

JOE (*to audience*). Tangiers! Four weeks of hashish and bum! Kenneth is already brightening . . .

HALLIWELL. Saw Nigel on the plane, with a woman!

NIGEL. Silly whore I picked up at customs. You didn't think I was a convert, did you?

JOE. I wondered.

NIGEL. Good God, no! I shall be taking it up the arse as usual for the next fortnight . . . See that one, she's got a prick that big.

HALLIWELL. Well, all I'd like to do to the creature is whip him.

JOE (*sotto voice to* HALLIWELL). Your psychological slip is showing.

NIGEL (*going, and as if to attract the attention of the one they have been ogling*). Er . . . Mohammad . . .

JOE (*to audience*). We went down to the beach early. We were hailed with 'hello' from a very beautiful sixteen year-old.

HALLIWELL. I want him.

BOY (*grinning*). Amis? Yes? Is good to have amis?

JOE. Wipe that silly grin off your face and put it on my arse.

BOY. 'Harse'?

HALLIWELL. Joe.

BOY. Parlez Francais?

HALLIWELL. Un peu . . . Eight years at school. I read better than parler. Do you know Simenon?

BOY. Simenon ami?

HALLIWELL. Tintin. I like Tintin . . . You know, le petit garcon avec le tuft of chevaux.

BOY. You want little boys?

HALLIWELL. No.

A silence.

JOE. Come to our apartment for tea this afternoon.

BOY. A trois heures?

JOE. Yes.

BOY. A bientôt.

HALLIWELL (*as the* BOY *goes*). Wasn't I good at arranging that?

JOE. I arranged it. You would have been standing there playing University Challenge all day. (*To audience.*) But Kenneth soon found a little Mohammad of his own. And it was four happy weeks to be spent with a succession of fourteen year-olds, all of whom seemed to be called Mohammad:

HALLIWELL. Mohammad Gold-Tooth.

JOE. Mohammad Sahara-Arse.

HALLIWELL. Mohammad G.

JOE. Mohammad Coppertone.

HALLIWELL. Mohammad Yellow-Shirt.

JOE. Mohammad Larbi.

HALLIWELL. Mohammad K.

JOE. Mohammad Y.

BOTH. Mohammad KY.

JOE. Mohammad . . . and so forth. I had sex with Mohammad Kiss-Me-Quick today, or at least I lay there and allowed him to fuck me, and I thought, as his prick shot in, that it was a most unappetising position for an internationally-known playwright to be in.

HALLIWELL. Piquant. P-Fucking-quant.

JOE (*to audience*). Dinner with George Greeves. He keeps up a constant stream of foul-mouthed commentary – nobody is spared. His chief target is the rich and pompous.

GREEVES (*large, fat and Australian*). I hate the fuckers. I'd like to line them up and shit on their faces . . . I gave a party once.

All the fucking queers for miles around flocked in. I believe we
even invited the Bishop of fucking London, but he had the piles
and couldn't come. Well, Auden, who'd been had when he was
fourteen, Auden was receiving the King's Gold Medal for Poetry
or some shit so said he might come late. 'Come when you like,'
I said, 'And we'll go round the Hammersmith Bridge afterwards
looking for a bit of young trade.' Well, in spite of the absence of
the Bishop and her fucking piles, we had a helluva time. Then
Wystan Hugh finally turned up. 'Ah, I've just come from one
George to another,' he said. 'The whole ceremony was a fiasco
really. I mean, George V wasn't all there at the best of times,
and he'd been given this bit of paper by Masefield – thank God
he's kicked it at last, been a disgrace to poetry for the last
ninety bleeding years – however the King had this bit of paper,
and said 'Now, Mr. Auden, I very much admired that poem
you wrote in 1926, and how are the boys?' Auden thought His
Majesty'd tumbled to the trade under Hammersmith Bridge.
Turns out the piece of paper said Auden had been a prep school
teacher. It really gave W.H. the shits for a minute or two, I can
tell you . . . (*As they raise their glasses.*) Well, here's wallaby
shite in your billabong.

EDNA WELTHORPE. Dear Mr. Kenneth Williams,
The people here leave a lot to be desired and flaunt their
preferences for what they cryptically call bits of the other at
every café. I might have been assaulted through the ears on
many occasions, by words only.
Yours, love and kisses, Edna.

JOE (*dictating to her*). P.S. Kenneth's having a marvellous time
too, which is a great help all round.

HALLIWELL. This happiness surely cannot last. We'll have to
pay for it. We'll be struck down from afar by disaster because
we're too happy.

JOE. To be young, good-looking, healthy, famous, comparatively
rich –

HALLIWELL. 'Comparatively' – you sold the *Loot* film rights for
twenty thousand!

JOE. Rich AND happy is surely going against nature. And when
one adds that daily I have the company of beautiful fifteen
year-old boys who find – for a small fee – fucking with me a

delightful sensation, no man can want for more.

HALLIWELL. The new play will be a disaster. We must sacrifice that in order that we may be spared disaster more intolerable.

They join NIGEL *in the café, other tourists are sitting nearby.*

JOE (*to audience*). At the beach café, two American heteros sat near us. (*They do so.*) So: he took it up the arse and afterwards thanked me for giving him such a good fucking. They're a most polite people. We've got a leopard skin rug in the flat and he wanted me to fuck him on that, only I'm afraid of the spunk, you see. It might adversely affect the spots.

NIGEL (*whispering*). They can hear you.

JOE. I mean them to. They have no right occupying chairs reserved for decent perverts. (*For the tourists again.*) He might bite a hole in the rug. It's the writhing he does. I can't ask him to control his excitement. It wouldn't be natural when you're six inches up the bum, would it?

The tourists stand and leave.

NIGEL. You shouldn't drive people away, the town needs tourists.

JOE. Not their kind, it doesn't. This is our town, our civilization. I want nothing to do with the civilization they made. It's not natural.

NIGEL. I really think, Joe, that you shouldn't bring nature into your conversation quite so often, you who have done more than anyone I know to outrage her.

JOE. I've never outraged nature. I've always listened to her advice and followed it wherever it went.

NIGEL. Well, if you ask me, that was a strange sort of joke.

JOE. It wasn't a joke. There's no such thing as a joke.

HALLIWELL. Well, this Arab-Israeli business is no joke either.

NIGEL. We'll be spat on in the streets. These people can turn so quickly.

HALLIWELL. There's to be a concentration camp for Europeans. We'll be interned.

NIGEL. Oh, my goodness, we'll be at the mercy of the brute commandants.

JOE (*to audience*). All the silly queens here are transferring their allegiance from the circumcised penis to the Secretary General of the United Nations. Fickle in their emotions.

M COPPERTONE. Hallo, Yusuf.

JOE. Coppertone!

M COPPERTONE. I come to say goodbye. I work now in Gibraltar. I am very happy.

JOE. And I am quite happy for you. (*To audience.*) I am quite sober and so my happiness is aided by relief that I will never see him again.

M COPPERTONE. Hey Yusuf . . . kiss me, I am so happy.

JOE (*to audience*). And I do so, feeling very happy for him and for all happiness, everywhere, however small. Because, of course, he will find only disillusion. But now, as I kiss him for the last time, we are, for different reasons, completely happy . . . But then he suddenly produced a gun.

M COPPERTONE. Hey, Yusuf!

JOE (*to audience*). I held up my hands.

M COPPERTONE (*shouting wildly*). I kill you!

He pulls the trigger and the gun harmlessly clicks. He laughs.

JOE (*to audience*). Any writer with an eye for the ironic would have had the gun loaded and the playwright of promise falling dead.

HALLIWELL. Nigel told me he'd had a little girl suck him off in a lift once.

GREEVES (*butting in*). Going down?

HALLIWELL. When the lift stopped, she picked his pocket and ran off.

GREEVES. Serves him right, the dirty old queen, for messing with the unclean ones. I am going to found a temple of my own. I'd have a tall penis on the high altar. And underneath we'd have a furnace for the prudish. We'd throw them down and the smoke would rise and wreath the glowing altar penis with glory.

Give the prick back its place in life.

JOE (*to audience*). I talked to a German girl called Vipsil. She is one of the most beautiful people I have ever met.

VIPSIL (*as she enters*). The Riviera is too crowded. In Greece they spit on us. Here, at least, the boys they talk, but don't touch.

JOE. Mohammad Larbi, who fancies himself as a lady killer, tried to pick her up on the beach. But like most Arabs, his technique left something to be desired.

LARBI (*to* VIPSIL). Hey, you, why you not speak? . . . You speak to Larbi. Larbi make good l'amour.

JOE (*to* VIPSIL). They're rather boring when they're trying to impress, aren't they?

VIPSIL. Yes . . .

JOE. Larbi, whose sense of his own attractiveness borders on the insane, could talk of nothing but Vipsil.

LARBI. Tomorrow I speak, then I fuck her.

JOE. I'll fuck her before you fuck her.

LARBI. Fifty dirhams, I fuck her.

JOE. OK. (*To audience*.) The next day, she and I went into the Casbah. How slow women walk.

VIPSIL. Islamic women are treated so bad.

JOE (*to himself*). The cow. How right the Arabs are about women.

VIPSIL. I cannot walk down the street without bad things being said.

JOE (*to audience*). I enjoyed the looks of envy as I walked along with her.

A street vendor offers her a silver chain.

VENDOR. You like? Two hundred dirham?

VIPSIL. Where does it go?

The VENDOR *begins to put it round her waist,* JOE *takes it from him and does it himself. They look at it on* VIPSIL. JOE *returns it to the street vendor and waves him away.*

JOE (*to audience*). He completely accepted me taking the

waistband from him, accepting also that she, whilst in my company, was my possession. And so, in fact, for the morning's walk around town, I possessed the most beautiful girl in Tangiers. I was curiously excited by this fact.

Torrential rain.

Pouring with rain. Tropical. Cypresses are sighing. (*To* HALLIWELL, *who is smoking hash.*) If the rain is coming down like this when Mohammad Flip-Flop arrives, it will be my dreams come true!

HALLIWELL (*stoned*). The kif is working.

JOE. You are, of course, well aware of my rain obsession. It's always in the rain that the soldier/engineer/apprentice/lorry-driver/master sergeant in the Marines fucks the schoolboy/errand boy/mentally defective farm labourer recently released from borstal.

HALLIWELL. But surely it does have to be in the back of a lorry or shed, though?

JOE. Yes . . . but with a fifteen year old boy and torrential rain, two-thirds of the fantasy is already a reality – the setting is of minor importance. The hashish was also beginning to work, so, as I had been warned not to do so, I had a double whisky . . . My lips felt as if they were made of rubber. The world became even more wonderful. Catching sight of myself in the mirror, I gazed, without self-consciousness, for perhaps five minutes, into my own eyes. I felt elated and danced a wild dance.

He does so. HALLIWELL *re-enters.*

HALLIWELL. Is this the farewell performance?

Enter FATIMA, *sweeping.*

JOE (*to audience*). The Fatima, who cleans our apartment, and steals the food at an alarming rate, yesterday gobbled a huge slice of hashish cake –

FATIMA *does so.*

which we had left purposely in the cupboard. An hour or so later, she fell silent and morose.

FATIMA. Malade.

JOE (*with a cordial smile*). That'll teach you to eat my food you thieving bitch.

FATIMA. Oui, monsieur.

JOE (*to audience*). Women are a terrible drag to have around. The Fatima stood staring at the wall in the kitchen for an hour. She did a little work and then disappeared into the garden leaving her yashmak and slippers upstairs.

HALLIWELL (*furious*). I'm going to put her things outside and go down to the beach.

JOE. Why?

HALLIWELL. Can't leave her in the house. She can have her cards.

JOE. It's hardly worth it. We're off to London day after tomorrow.

HALLIWELL *nevertheless puts the clothes outside, then joins* NIGEL.

HALLIWELL. I've taught our Fatima a lesson. Joe wanted to ignore her, but she's got to be taught a lesson.

NIGEL. How right you are, dear. It takes a woman to deal with a woman.

JOE. If I'd said that you'd be on a charter flight to London by now.

NIGEL (*pointing off*). Look at the package on that one.

NIGEL *goes.*

HALLIWELL. That's Larbi. (*To* JOE.) He'll do anything.

JOE. How do you know? You've only asked him to do so little.

HALLIWELL. Oh, all the boys will do anything.

JOE. They won't. There's a lot of things he won't do. You yourself said he wouldn't take it. It was your excuse for choosing him in the first place.

HALLIWELL. You're selfish. You can't bear it if you're not the centre of attention. You continually sneer at me for being masturbated. Does fucking little boys make you virile? (*At which,* HALLIWELL *starts attacking* JOE, *throwing him to the*

ground . . . then, when he has calmed.) I saw you in Nigel's car
and I've never seen you at a distance before. I thought 'what a
long-nosed ponce.' When we get back to London, we're
finished. This is the end!

JOE. I wonder you didn't add 'I'm going back to Mother!'

HALLIWELL. That's the kind of line that makes your plays
ultimately worthless.

JOE (*to audience*). It went on and on until I put out the light.

June 30th

JOE (*to audience*). We landed in London without further mishap.

HALLIWELL. How dead everyone in London looks. The party's
over.

JOE (*to audience*). I feel the need for something fresh. Not work,
though I shall finish 'The Butler', just a change of scene. Even
a month of sex with teenage boys becomes monotonous. Ecstasy
is as liable to bore as boredom. (*To* HALLIWELL, *who is
looking morose.*) In Tangiers you were all smiles, three hours in
London and you're the Ghost of Christmas Past.

HALLIWELL. Joe, we must talk.

JOE. Alright, what do you want? (*To audience.*) But then Miss
Boynes came barging in, to make her farewells:

BOYNES. Well, I'm really moving. I leave on the twenty-first to
take up residence in Holland-on-Sea. My new bungalow's
centrally heated throughout. Every room heated from all points.
I've left the door of my cupboard in the shed. I took it off to
make room –

JOE (*not that* MISS BOYNES *stops for* JOE *to say to the audience*).
She seemed to be talking nonsense out of relief.

BOYNES. For my fridge. Which I'm leaving behind. The builder
down there's put a blue handle on my front door. It's a yellow
front door as well. Looked most out of place. Very common.

HALLIWELL. Very common.

BOYNES. Still, there it is, I shall soon have that altered. And the
builder is most pleased with everything. He told me 'There's
plenty of whist drives and bridge. We're a merry community.'

(*She laughs.*) He seemed to think I was the artistic type. Well, I let him think so. It's not lies, is it? I've told the estate agent I've left the keys with you. I don't want him to get onto the Cordens. My word, he'd have a shock. Do you think you could possibly – ?

JOE. Mrs. Corden broke the light switch outside your door, fiddling with it.

BOYNES. Oh, I see. Yes, very well, then. I suppose I shall have to pay for it to be done myself . . .

July 13th

HALLIWELL. I wish I'd stayed in Morocco. Oh, this terrible city! Let's look for a place in Brighton.

JOE. I'm not languishing down there.

HALLIWELL. We need a change of scene. Somewhere quiet and healthy.

JOE. OK, then, look. But I'm not selling this flat.

HALLIWELL. Why? We've been talking about moving for years.

JOE. I need a London base. For rehearsals.

HALLIWELL. For your London pick-ups. You'll bring them back here, won't you?

JOE. You know I didn't mean that.

HALLIWELL. No, but it's what you'll do, isn't it?

JOE. If you won't talk sense, I'll find someone who will. (*To audience.*) In the Holloway Road toilet, I stood next to a Greek Cypriot. Very stupid looking.

CYPRIOT. Come to the park. I shag you.

JOE. An ice-cream seller's accent. When we got to the park it seemed as though I'd met a maniac.

CYPRIOT. See over there, two men, they shag. And there. A man and a girl. They shag, perhaps. Everybody shag: please let me shag you! I be quick!

JOE (*to* THE CYPRIOT). But we're in the light.

CYPRIOT. Naw, nobody notice.

JOE. Up against a tree, he fucked me. He was quick.

CYPRIOT. I shag a boy last week. I pay him two pound. You don't want money, do you?

JOE (*to* THE CYPRIOT). No, I've plenty of money.

CYPRIOT. Me too. I've plenty of money. Too many people shag here. Maybe next time we shag in a room. Maybe next time you shag me as well.

JOE. My pleasure.

July 15th

JOE (*to* HALLIWELL, *reading his play*). Well, what do you think? (HALLIWELL *laughs*.) What?

HALLIWELL. The ending.

JOE. Did you get the Euripidean reference?

HALLIWELL. Of course I got it. I studied the Classics, remember?

JOE. I don't suppose the critics will.

HALLIWELL. The Sergeant's dress should be leopard skin. It'll give it the right Dionysian image.

JOE. Yeah. Terrific. I never thought of that. (*He scribbles it down*.) You'll be seeing it.

HALLIWELL. I usually do.

JOE. I'm going to start something new now. That farce about Edward VII. I'll call it 'Prick Up Your Ears'. I hope my play'll be worthy of your title.

HALLIWELL. Please don't condescend to me. Just don't.

JOE (*to audience*). Went to the matinée for a bit of peace and quiet. In the foyer, two old women were talking.

The following scene is the sadder for being played in a truly cheerful way.

EDITH. May? May Hallet! Is that you?

MAY. Yes, it's me . . . Edith! You know I'm nearly deaf now.

EDITH. No, I'm nearly blind myself.

MAY. Yes, next Thursday.

EDITH. I can hardly see anything, and I'm worried for fear people will think I'm cutting them.

MAY (*sternly*). You don't want that.

JOE (*to audience*). Although she was very old, you could see she had been a lesbian once.

EDITH. You must come and see my new flat. I've got a cat. It's just like a dog. I've always had dogs and this is my first cat. I'm so pleased it's just like a dog.

MAY. Are you working?

EDITH. No, I'm looking for work. I haven't worked for nearly a month. I'll take anything – radio, television, films.

MAY. What about theatre?

EDITH. Oh, theatre, too. But there simply isn't anything for me.

MAY. You don't want to say that.

EDITH. Are you working?

MAY. I'm too old, yes, I'm really too old.

JOE (*to audience*). She had arthritis and red carpet slippers on.

EDITH. Now, May, don't forget to ring me. I shall look forward to seeing you and showing you my cat. His name is Shep.

July 16th

JOE (*to* HALLIWELL). Are you going to stand in front of that mirror all day?

HALLIWELL. I've been washing your fucking underpants. That's why I've been at the sink.

JOE. Please don't let the whole neighbourhood know you're a queen.

HALLIWELL. You know I suffer from hay fever, and you deliberately get on my nerves.

JOE. I'm going out today, I can't stand much more of it.

HALLIWELL. Go out then. I don't want you in here. (*As his voice trails off.*) You're never here these days anyway.

JOE (*to audience*). Nobody around to pick up. Only a lot of disgusting old men. I shall be a disgusting old man myself one day. But I have high hopes of dying in my prime.

July 20th

WILLIAMS. And there was this party who'd been to see *Loot* and the woman came up to me and said 'You're in that play *Loot*, aren't you?' 'Yes,' I said. 'Disgusting play,' she said, 'it's all about pregnant women and Jesus Christ, and we know all about them. I walked out half-way through. What happened at the finish?' 'By walking out, Madam,' I said, 'you forfeited the right to know.' Marvellous reply, wasn't it?

JOE. Marvellous.

WILLIAMS. 'Ere, did you hear about Martin. Well, Lilly Law finally picked him up. Gave her the choice of gaol or a mental home. She chose the mental home. 'Well,' she said, 'there's all the lovely mental cock I'm sure it'll be very gay.' Well, she went into the mental home and they gave her all these drugs to stop her thinking like a queen. Within three months, he was so depressed he's committed suicide. Poor cow.

July 21st

WILLIAMS. To Peter Willes' for dinner.

JOE. Bill Naughton told me how much he admired *Loot*. But you see, Nichola, I've never liked anything he's written, I can't be generous. I can't return praise with any degree of conviction. I'd like to think I'd be as nice to somebody if I admired their writing. But who could it be?

HALLIWELL. God.

WILLES (*horrified*). That's an old Etonian tie!

HALLIWELL. Yes, it's a joke. I'm sending up Eton.

WILLES. You're just pathetic. It's disgraceful wearing that tie.

HALLIWELL. It's a joke.

WILLES. People won't know.

HALLIWELL. The people I meet, they'll think it's funny.

WILLES. You'll make people angry.

HALLIWELL. I don't care. I want them to be angry.

WILLES. But why? People dislike you enough already. Why make them more angry? It's permissible, although silly, as a foible of youth, but you – a middle-aged nonentity – it's sad and pathetic.

JOE. Now stop this both of you. It's ridiculous to carry on this way over a wretched tie. What do you think of my new play?

HALLIWELL. You'll hate it.

WILLES. Why?

HALLIWELL. All you people that are mad on Joe really have no idea what he's like.

WILLES. I'm not mad on Joe, whatever do you mean?

NICHOLA (*breaking the embarrassed silence*). Joe, it's the very best thing you've done so far.

WILLES. It's so exciting, it's like a Palais Royale farce.

HALLIWELL. He only likes it because I said he wouldn't.

July 23rd

JOE. Look, sharing of any kind means an invasion of privacy. I need to be utterly free.

HALLIWELL. Love is involvement. You can't live without love.

JOE. There are many definitions of love. It depends on your point of view. You can love your work and be entirely committed to the pursuit of perfection. I need promiscuity. I need to be the fly on the wall.

HALLIWELL. A home should have the stability of a loyal relationship.

JOE. You sound like a heterosexual.

HALLIWELL. You can only love properly if it's for one person or for God.

JOE. You must do whatever you like as long as you enjoy it and don't hurt anyone else. Get yourself fucked if you want to. (JOE *gradually starts to address the audience rather than* HALLIWELL.) Get yourself anything you like. When you're dead you'll regret not having fun with your genital organs. Fuck Judeo-Christian Society!

July 26th

Meanwhile, HALLIWELL *is visiting a doctor.*

HALLIWELL. He says I'm a thorn in his side. I can't help it. I'm so angry. Everything I do comes out angry. Things have been so much worse since our holiday. They should have been better. He stays away as much as he can. It's terrible when he's not there. I get so worried. Then I get angry at him for making me worry. Then I just worry.

DOCTOR. I prescribed valium the last time. Seventh of May.

HALLIWELL. They don't help much. I still can't sleep. The pains in my chest have come back.

DOCTOR. We talked about that. (*He is trying to imply the pain is psychosomatic.*)

HALLIWELL. They still hurt though. I hurt. I AM a middle-aged nonentity. Every call is for him. Every letter is for him. Every question, when we're out, is for him. Everything I say or feel is his. He writes it down in his Diary. I'm just 'Kenneth Halliwell'. Like some stranger. We've been everything to each other. When I met him, he was eighteen and I was twenty-five, though God knows, I looked middle-aged even then. There's nothing he's written, hardly anything he's ever done in his adult life that hasn't involved me. (*Pause.*) Except the trade. I hate the trade. I hate all that.

DOCTOR. Maybe that's why he does it.

HALLIWELL. He does it because he enjoys it. And because I don't satisfy him.

DOCTOR. He knows how you feel about his . . .?

HALLIWELL. Yes.

DOCTOR. And writes it down in his diary? While you're in the room?

HALLIWELL. Some of it's very funny. He's a good writer.

DOCTOR. He leaves it where you can read it?

HALLIWELL. In a drawer.

DOCTOR. Locked?

HALLIWELL. No.

DOCTOR. Even though he knows you're threatened and repulsed by his sexual escapades?

HALLIWELL. . . . Yes.

Pause.

DOCTOR. Do you think he's trying to tell you something?

HALLIWELL. What?

DOCTOR (*slightly irritated by* HALLIWELL's *self-blindness*). Do you think he might be trying to force you to leave him?

HALLIWELL. I am going to leave him. I'm going to leave him and then I'm going to kill myself. I can't live with him. I don't want to live without him.

The DOCTOR *is writing a prescription.*

You think he's using the Diary to taunt me?

DOCTOR. I'm prescribing Largactil and Tofranil. They'll help with the anger. I'm going to make an appointment for you to see a psychiatrist at St. Bernard's. I'll call you with the details.

Exit HALLIWELL. THE DOCTOR *dials the 'phone.*

Hello, Douglas here. I've just seen a patient who seems suicidal. He insisted on seeing me without an appointment. I think you should see him. Yes. Homosexual. Yes. Clinging. Bit of a pain, really. Will you see him?

July 27th

HALLIWELL. I don't want to go to Brighton. I don't want to spend a weekend with the Lewensteins.

JOE. Oscar specifically invited you.

HALLIWELL. I'm just an extra in your epic.

JOE. Look, we've got to make plans for *What the Butler Saw.*

So HALLIWELL *gets up to go to Brighton.*

LEWENSTEIN. I have this mad idea of doing it with Binkie and getting the Haymarket.

Throughout this scene, all HALLIWELL's *remarks are ignored by the other two, and frequently interrupted.*

HALLIWELL. Theatre of Perfection!

LEWENSTEIN. When the curtain goes up, you should feel you're right back in the old theatre of Reassurance.

JOE. Roses? French windows?

LEWENSTEIN. Exactly.

HALLIWELL. Alistair Sim would be excellent as Rance.

LEWENSTEIN. What do you think of Ralph Richardson?

JOE. Well, if he would . . .

HALLIWELL. Years too old. And not noted for his comic performances. Arthur Lowe is a possibility.

LEWENSTEIN. Ralph told Binkie he'd love to do a play of yours.

JOE. Really?

LEWENSTEIN. The Lord Chamberlain almost certainly won't allow the references to Mr. Churchill, will he?

JOE. It's only a statue referred to.

LEWENSTEIN. He won't be too pleased. Not to mention the laws of libel.

JOE. What am I saying about Churchill though?

HALLIWELL. You're saying he had a big prick.

JOE. That isn't libellous, surely? I wouldn't sue anyone for saying I had a big prick. No man would. In fact, I might pay them to do it. (*To audience.*) Kenneth and I went for a thoroughly unpleasant walk. We had to clamber over breakwaters thick with slime and grime. The sea frothed and bubbled with the rain and an overpowering smell of chemicals, rotting seaweed, and the dung of countless birds met us.

HALLIWELL. This is a terrible way to spend our leisure.

JOE. Look at that boy! England is intolerable. I'd be able to fuck that in an Arab country. I could take him home and stick my cock up him.

HALLIWELL. Joe, this is just verbal exhibitionism.

JOE. I hate this tight-arsed civilization. I find lust

indistinguishable from anger. I get angry when I see something
I can't have.

HALLIWELL. We must get back to Tangiers as soon as possible.
Let's take a flat, unfurnished. We could be there now. Instead
of this wilderness.

JOE (*to audience*). When we got back, Oscar's mother:

MRS. LEWENSTEIN. Did you have a nice walk?

HALLIWELL (*trying*). . . . Yes.

MRS. LEWENSTEIN. I can't stand in a lift, you know, without
thinking of the gas chambers.

HALLIWELL. . . . Terrible.

MRS. LEWENSTEIN. And people ask why Jews went to their
deaths without complaining.

HALLIWELL. In some circumstances, you can't fight back.

MRS. LEWENSTEIN. And now this way. Six days! Why are the
Egyptians so against Israel? Surely it's wrong. They've worked
so hard cultivating the desert. It was barren, you know, just a
patch of scrub. And now they tell me it's so wonderful.

HALLIWELL. All green fields.

MRS. LEWENSTEIN. All green and fertile.

JOE. I wondered idly what would happen if I interfered with
Oscar's children.

He moves away.

July 28th

(*To audience*). After walking through most of Hove –

HALLIWELL (*who has now managed to detach himself from* MRS.
LEWENSTEIN, *and is staring at* JOE). Joe!

JOE (*who goes on addressing the audience, completely oblivious of*
HALLIWELL's *interruption*). I did find a gents. There was a
man there, tall, grand, and smiling. In the gloom, he looked
aristocratic. When the lights were turned on, I could see he was
stupid, smiling and bank-clerkish. He showed his cock. I let
him feel mine. (*To* CLERKISH MAN.) You have a place?

CLERKISH MAN. No, I don't have the choice of my neighbours, you see. They're down on me and I can't take the risk. He'll suck you off though. I've seen him do it.

He indicates 'rather as one who hails a taxi'.

JOE (*to audience*). A dwarfish creature. The dwarf sucked me off while the other man smiled benevolently and then went back to his neighbours refreshed.

August 1st

JOE (*to audience*). Off to Leicester this morning to see a production of 'Sloane'. Kenneth seemed odd. I asked him to come with me.

HALLIWELL (*looking surprised*). No.

JOE *goes.* HALLIWELL, *now in the depths of clinical depression, slowly takes the diary out of the drawer and looks through it. He puts it back in the drawer.*

A pause.

August 2nd

BALLANTINE (*addressing audience, as does every character now, except* JOE *and* HALLIWELL). Kenneth came to see me at the Criterion about a week before he killed Joe.

HALLIWELL. I brought you the book you wanted. The Muggeridge.

BALLANTINE. I'd never discussed wanting the book.

HALLIWELL. I'm very depressed. I think I'm having a breakdown. I've had them before, you know. I can't go on suffering like this.

WILLES. Halliwell thought he was losing Joe, but he never would have.

BALLANTINE. I asked him if he'd seen a doctor.

HALLIWELL. He gave me purple hearts. Nothing helps. Not even the Samaritans. I went there on my way here. They're no good. All they do is make you cups of tea.

BALLANTINE. I took him for a drink after the show.

HALLIWELL. It was me that got Joe to write. *Loot* was my title. Everyone thinks Joe's the creative one. But I created Joe.

MRS. CORDEN. They argued a lot in the last few weeks. I had to buy earplugs.

BALLANTINE. I had never met Kenneth on his own, and upset. He was obsessed about the middle-aged nonentity dig.

HALLIWELL. Joe's new play is brilliant. At the end, the policeman comes through the skylight dressed in a leopard-skin dress. Gives it a Euripidean ending. I thought of that. And what he says when the ladder comes down: 'We are now approaching what some of our racier novelists term the climax'. 'Climax' is the Greek for ladder. That's me. I gave Joe his Classical education.

BALLANTINE. I invited him to come and stay until Joe got back from Leicester.

HALLIWELL. I'll be alright, he's back tomorrow teatime.

DOCTOR. Ten o'clock on the Eighth was the last time I spoke to Kenneth. I rang him from the surgery. He said he was not too bad, he said 'Don't worry, I'll go to see the psychiatrist on Wednesday morning.' 'Are you sure?' I said. He was rather put out I was going on holiday. He was such a . . . wet person. I never thought he'd have the courage to kill himself, let alone batter Orton to death.

BALLANTINE. They came in together that night. Kenneth was very much stranger.

JOE (*to* BALLANTINE). You wouldn't believe how she played Kath. Carried her sex around like a poodle behind her. Here, you're Sloane, I'm Kath.

JOE *gropes* BALLANTINE.

'You should wear more clothes, Mr. Sloane. I believe you're as naked as me.'

HALLIWELL (*very shut-off*). I went to the Samaritans. And I . . .

BALLANTINE. Yes, I know.

HALLIWELL. I went to the Samaritans. They're no good, they only give you cups of tea. They said I was –

JOE. Oh, you told her all that, did you?

BALLANTINE (*apart*). I thought he obviously doesn't know
Kenneth's been ill, or he wouldn't be mucking around like this.

JOE (*to* BALLANTINE). So she's rubbing up against him like
this . . .

He gropes BALLANTINE *again.*

BALLANTINE (*to audience*). I thought, My God. He can't see.
He hasn't noticed.

*As the lights slowly dim, 'A Day in the Life' from the 'Sergeant
Pepper' album fades up.*

The tableau: JOE *continues to grope* BALLANTINE, *everyone else
is looking at* HALLIWELL.

They slowly fade from view. And as the music peaks, total blackout.